THE SACRIFICIAL PIG

by Kammie Minor

Illustrated by Julie Ibarra

Copyright © 2023 by Kammie Minor

All Rights Reserved.

Illustrations by Julie Ibarra
Formatting provided by Trisha Fuentes

No part of this book may be reproduced in any form or by any electronic or mechanical means, including information storage and retrieval systems, without written permission from the author, except for the use of brief quotations in a book review.

ISBN: 979-8-9891821-1-4 (Paperback)
        979-8-9891821-2-1 (Ebook)
        979-8-9891821-0-7 (Hardcover)

Dedicated to Children of All Ages

NOTES

NOTES

Pigs are one of the many animals God created! They are very intelligent and have been known to be smarter than a three-year-old child.

Pigs are also very calm and peaceful animals. In fact, they rarely get upset unless they feel threatened by another animal or human. For example, a mother pig will get very upset and charge toward the one that is trying to harm any of her babies.

There are many stories of pigs that play a role in saving the lives of children and animals from drowning.

A farmer told a story about one of his pigs he saw running toward a boy crying out for help. His pig jumped into the water, pulled the boy out by his shirt, saving him from drowning. The farmer was so amazed as he watched his pig save the little boy's life.

A similar story was told about a baby fawn that had fallen into the river while getting a drink of water.
A pig heard its cry for help and saved it by pulling it out of the river. These stories show just how compassionate and intelligent pigs really are, and it looks like they are very good swimmers too!

One day, a man held one of his pigs high up in the air, and it started squealing and wiggling around so much that it almost wiggled right out of his hands. When he put it back on the ground, it calmed down and stopped squealing. So, are pigs afraid of heights? It sure sounds like it.

While you are reading the rest of this book, think about what you have just learned about pigs.

One day, Jesus and His disciples were headed to the other side of the Sea of Galilee. When Jesus got out of the boat, a man with evil spirits ran to meet Him and fell at His feet.

Jesus loved this man and knew he was being controlled by demons. He lived in the caves where the dead are buried, and he would often scream day and night on the hills cutting himself with stones.
The demons inside this man did not want him to live.

Many times people from his town would put chains on his hands and feet trying to keep him from hurting himself. But this man was very strong and would break the chains into pieces. Nobody was strong enough to control him or hold him down.

They also knew that Jesus would make them leave this man. So, they asked Jesus, "what do you want with us?" Jesus then asked the evil spirits their name. They answered and said "Legion," which means there are many of them.

Meanwhile, there was a large herd of pigs feeding nearby. All of the pigs together totaled about 2000.

NOW THAT IS A LOT OF PIGS!

They begged Him to send them into the pigs because they didn't want to be cast out and sent to the abyss where they are from. But Jesus was aware of their plans and knew it would fail them.

Jesus then commanded the evil spirits to go and leave the man, and He sent them into the pigs.

Since pigs are calm and peaceful animals, they knew right away the evil spirits had entered them. So, they ran very fast to the cliff, jumped off into the lake, and drowned. Because the pigs sacrificed their lives by drowning, the evil spirits had to go back to the abyss, and they were not able to return to the man again.

The pigs in this story are only a demonstration of what Jesus sacrificed for us on the cross. Without Jesus, we are like the man in chains waiting to be set free. So, if you haven't already, run as fast as the pigs did and ask Jesus to come into your heart today! Then, get a bible that is easy for you to read so you can learn more about Who God is and what He has planned for those who believe in Christ Jesus. Here are a few bible verses that reference who we are and what we have in Jesus: Matt 11:27, 28:18; John 3:35; Eph 1: 20-22; Heb 1:3; I John 1:9, 3:16, 5:18.

Kammie Minor is a homeschool mom and former Dental Hygienist in Texas. Due to covid 19 in 2020, her career in Dental hygiene was put on hold and her relationship with Jesus grew as she had more time to spend studying the Word of God. As she was reading Mark 5: 1-20, she wondered if there was something significant about the pigs in the story. After researching and discovering how intelligent they are, she knew how important they were to this story. She was inspired by the Holy Spirit to write this book so other children and families can have fun while learning what we have in Jesus. She hopes this develops child-like-faith that the Bible tells us about in Matt 18:2-4; Jesus called a little child to Him and put the child among them. Then He said, "I tell you the truth, unless you turn from your sins and become like little children, you will never get into the Kingdom of Heaven. So anyone who becomes as humble as this little child is the greatest in the Kingdom of Heaven." NLT.

NOTES

NOTES

www.ingramcontent.com/pod-product-compliance
Lightning Source LLC
Chambersburg PA
CBHW040725060526
44119CB00083B/327